Courts of Air and Earth

Poetry by Trevor Joyce

New Writers' Press, Dublin
Sole Glum Trek
Watches
Pentahedron
The Poems of Sweeny Peregrine
stone floods

Form Books, London
Hellbox

Wild Honey Press, Bray, Co. Wicklow
Syzygy
Without Asylum

The Gig, Willowdale, Ont., Canada
(Takeover) Undone, Say
Takeover (Undone, Say)

Shearsman Books, Exeter / New Writers' Press, Dublin
with the first dream of fire they hunt the cold
— A Body of Work 66/00 —

Motivex, Poznan / New Writers' Press, Dublin
Dwory Powietrza i Ziemi

The Gig, Willowdale, Ont., Canada / New Writers' Press, Dublin
What's in Store

TREVOR JOYCE

Courts of Air and Earth

Shearsman Books
Exeter

First published in the United Kingdom in 2008 by
Shearsman Books Ltd
58 Velwell Road
Exeter EX4 4LD

ISBN 978-0-907562-95-5

Acknowledgements
'The Poems of Sweeny, Peregrine' first appeared in the book of the
same name, published by New Writers' Press, Dublin in 1976, and was
subsequently collected in the author's *with the first dream of fire they hunt
the cold* (Shearsman Books, Exeter / New Writers' Press, 2001; 2nd edition,
2003), and in *Dwory Powietrza i Ziemi* (Motivex, Poznan / New Writers'
Press). The 'Love Songs from a Dead Tongue' first appeared in *Masthead*
and in *Poetry Ireland Review*, and were subsequently collected in *Dwory
Powietrza i Ziemi* and in *What's in Store* (The Gig, Willowdale, Ont. /
New Writers' Press, 2007). The 'Anonymous Love Songs from the Irish'
previously appeared in *Take Over* (The Gig, 2003), and *What's in Store* (The
Gig / New Writers' Press, 2007). 'Cry Help' was first collected in *stone floods*
(New Writers' Press, 1995), and subsequently in *with the first dream of fire
they hunt the cold* (2001; 2003).

Author photograph by Jason Lee, reproduced with permission.
Cover photograph by Trevor Joyce.

Contents

Foreword

These renditions of early Irish poetry cut to the quick. They are wild things, ravaged, and empty of sentimentality, but all heart. I think the key to their force is that they are based in syntax and sound. They move word by word, rather than by phrasing, and so it is the relationship between the words that holds the stanzas (heartbeats) together, not a rush of sentiment. They mediate between tradition and modernity.

Tradition would hold that music expresses a single culture's necessity, the strain of the voice to sing it. Traditionally, speech aspires to song and wants to contain and order the raw lonely voice, to gather it back into a communal texture that is recognizable to all.

Modernity abandons the community in favor of a plurality of interpretations. The fusing of these two approaches to language can only be accomplished by locating the impersonal strain in each line of the poem. The impersonal saves the translation from history.

This is what Trevor Joyce has done in these magnificent poems. They are Celtic in their cells and bones, their knowing of landscape as an interior, while weather and consciousness are a single phenomenon of the outside. Yet the spare syntactical arrangements are also modern in their alienation from comfort zones. Nothing quite adds up.

The beginning of culture is the end of it too. These poems prove that point. They are magnificent in the deepest meaning of the word.

Fanny Howe

The
Poems
of
Sweeny,
Peregrine:

A
Working
of the
Corrupt
Irish Text
(1966–76)

It's no secret how Sweeny, king of Dal Araidhe and scion of noble though disputed stock, wandered deranged from battle. These periods recount his flight, its reasons and results. These are the records of Sweeny's madness.

There was then in Ireland a cleric called Ronan Finn. A pious and temperate man, he was dedicated to serving his God and opposing the forces of evil.

A time came when he began to plot a church which fell within the area of Dal Araidhe, Sweeny's domain. As the monk circled the boundaries of his site he made such a racket with his hand-bell that it wasn't long before Sweeny had inquired the source of the strange tolling, and, in a great rage, set out to put an end to Ronan's building. Eorann, his wife, tried to restrain him by grabbing the crimson tassels of his cloak. The fibula sprang from his throat and its precious metal clattered on the floor. His cloak fell limp in the queen's hand as Sweeny made for the church. As yet, only his nakedness was stark.

When Sweeny arrived he found Ronan enumerating the manifold epithets of God from his best psalter. Sweeny snatched that book and tossed it far out into the nearby lake where it tumbled swiftly down the chill waters. Next, as he got set to haul Ronan from the church, he was interrupted by a sudden cry; a servant had arrived from Congal Claon requiring Sweeny to fight at Magh Rath. Left alone as Sweeny and the messenger departed, Ronan bemoaned the loss of his psalter, and recalled with rancour his humiliation.

After a day and a night, a convenient otter fished the psalter up from the bed of the lake and brought it to Ronan. The monk inspected the book and, when he found it intact, began at once to praise God and curse Sweeny, saying: "pray God, naked as Sweeny came let him remain until a spear puts end to such extravagant flight." Then he cursed all Sweeny's kinsfolk; only Eorann was excused, and came in for a blessing.

Ronan next made his way towards Magh Rath, hoping to secure a pact between Domhnall and the tribe of Congal. He did not succeed in this aim; the best he could do was to arrange a truce each night between certain hours. But always the truce was broken; each morning before the hour of battle Sweeny would kill one of Domhnall's men, and he would kill another after the combat ceased at night.

On the day fixed for the deciding battle, Sweeny was first in the field. His skin gleamed through a silken shirt belted with satin. He wore the tunic Congal gave him the day he bested Oilill Cedach; crimson thickly bordered with gold. Chips of carbuncle gemmed its edge and bright silver buttons glinted through loops of silk. Broad heads of iron shod his twin lances, and a shield of tough yellow horn hung at his back. The haft of the sword was worked in gold.

When the other warriors had arrived, and all the great forces were gathered there, Ronan began to go among them with the psalmists of his community. They sprinkled holy water over the assembled ranks and Sweeny received its benefits along with his comrades. Suspicious of being mocked, he slipped his finger through the loop of his iron-tipped spear and with a single blow he killed one of the psalmists. He made another cast then; this time the target of his lance was the monk himself. The blade penetrated the bell on the monk's breast, but the shaft ricochetted, jolting vertically up. Then Ronan spoke: "I invoke the might of God," he said, "that just as that shaft flew high among the upper vapours, you may go also, birdlike, and may your death be by a spear as your spear killed my ward. My curse on you and my blessing on Eorann; and may all the ancient powers bedevil your kin and offspring."

Then the battle was joined. As the vast armies clashed, the warriors grunted and roared, and three times they raised a cry like the loud challenge of a stag, answered and echoed. When

Sweeny heard this shrill cacophany rebounding toward him from all sides so that even the sun shook and reverberated in the heavens, he looked up. Troubled then, rage and dread began to grow in him and he became dizzy and a strange restlessness seized him. All the places he knew seemed suddenly repulsive now, and he longed to arrive where he had never been. His fingers trembled and his pulse rushed in his ears as he swayed on weakening legs. His sight was distorted and all his senses dulled when he fulfilled the curse of Ronan. Deranged and rattled as a wild bird, Sweeny began his wanderings.

This commencement of his flight did not disturb even the glittering dew that hung upon the grass; still, crystalline, it lingered. He did not halt on pastureland or rock, in haggard, moor, or dense timber, all of which he passed in that initial flight, but entered the yew-tree of Ros Bearaigh.

Sweeny's kinsmen were routed. It was when their diminished forces passed in their retreat the yew-tree of Ros Bearaigh and tried to cajole him out with promises of wealth that Sweeny, crimson-cloth, whose hair matched the blond adze-flakes, and whose eyes were as blue and flawless ice, rejected them: "you do not know me."

He sprang from the tree into the blind alleys of the rainclouds, remote from roofs and mountains, then travelled Ireland, ferreting chine and gorge, grazing the high jagged cordons of the ivy and tight fissures of stone, from estuary to estuary, among summits and valleys and their recurrence, until he reached the genial Glen Bolcain. Here is the resort of the Irish-turned-maniac, and the glen delights them. Pannage is underfoot, berries abound, and there are many and sweet springs. In simple joy the innocent mad would strike each other down for a choice sprig of cress or a niche to sleep in.

Sweeny dawdled in the glen till one night when he roosted high in an ivy-strangled whitethorn. He couldn't sleep there because each time he twitched the wood tines stuck him, leaving his flesh split and specked with blood. So he went to where a single blackthorn limb spired above a briary thicket, rayed with fine spikes. He perched there, but the slender branch sagged under him and it snapped, throwing him into the thorny mass below so that his skin from heel to head was a crimson tracery. It was thus that Sweeny took a scunner against thorns.

The period of Sweeny's peregrinations between this grievous issuing from Glen Bolcain and his return thereto, was seven years. It was his fastness and his den; women there did not, through thrashing of the yellow flax, recall to him his kinsfolks' thrashing at Magh Rath. Only random care had power to expel him.

Soon in search of him came Loingseachan, a man of close, if uncertain, relation. Beyond any question, though, was his concern for Sweeny, for three times he had retrieved him from out the tortuous courses of his madness. Loingseachan now sought him in the glen, sought him by his prints beside the cress-providing springs, and by the hail of small timber with which his aërial disquietude threatened the timid fauna of the earth. But it was Sweeny who first sighted his pursuer, when he found him asleep in the glen, and he chanted over him the bitter threnodies of his madness.

Shortly the pursuit was resumed with ruse and lure, and Sweeny had occasion in his flight to regret the curse of Ronan Finn. He had recourse to the company of his wife Eorann, whom that cleric had blessed, but he found no haven there. Eorann had taken for husband one Guaire, and the henchmen of this feeble thug drove Sweeny back into the darkness and the frost of which he had made such desperate and formal complaint. The wife of a local erenagh attempted then to beguile him, but shrewdly he eluded her, bidding her tend to her husband and her glebe, and calling to mind their common end. The sharpness of her eyes had troubled him.

He went then to one of the refuges he retained in his home-land, and entered the yew-tree of Ros Earcain. For a month he lived there undetected, but once more there came against him the wily Loingseachan. That man, captor elect, approached the yew, lifting his eyes to the distraught figure on the boughs above. "Sweeny," he began, "I find you here starved, naked on a branch as any bird, with parched lips and a clenched arse. It is hard that this should be the end of one whose body thrilled to silk and dull tunics of satin; once you loosed flickering reins across the necks of foreign stallions, your house held noble youths, fine gentlemen, choice hounds and mastercraftsmen. You dined at many mansions, and countless lords, leaders, squires and hos-pitallers noted your every whim. Quondam owner of many goblets, with cruets of carved horn for liquors dry and sweet: bird-form now, glimpsed only between wilderness and wilder-ness. It is hard." At this, Sweeny lingered. He asked for news of his kinsfolk, and Loingseachan, eloquent in his deceit, told him that both his parents were dead, his brother also, and his wife. "A house without a wife," said Sweeny, "is a rudderless boat, is a coat of feathers to the skin, is the kindling of a single fire."

"Dead is your daughter."

"The heart's needle is an only daughter."

"And your only son is dead."

At this last, Sweeny tumbled from the tree and fell to the gyves and shackles of his pursuer.

Locks and fetters were fitted on him and remained, until at last, through manacle and spancel, sense returned. Memory and rea-son returned to him, as did his figure and appearance; kingship was manifest in him.

When the season of harvest came round, Loingseachan went with his people into the fields. Not so, Sweeny. He was locked deep in an inner chamber of the mill with only the mill-hag for company and warden, and she had been enjoined to silence lest she unsettle the frail sanity of the man. Wilfully, she spoke, inquiring the exploits of his madness. He cursed her, but she led him on, saying the truth should out. She goaded him to leap then; first, over the bed-rail. She matched that. Next through the rooflight of the chamber she followed him, and across the five cantreds of Dal Araidhe, until wearily he roosted on an ivy-branch in Fiodh Gaibhle, the hag beside him.

It was the end of the harvest-time precisely. The cry of the hunt and the bellow of the running stag carried through the wood; Sweeny suppressed his initial fright and chanted of the trees of Ireland, and of his grief.

This done, he took off once more across the summits of the land, and each leap was mimicked by the hag until at last he sprang from the battlements of Dun Sobairce and she faltered in pursuit; she fell upon the sea-cliffs and the rock broke her. A catspaw played with her wreck.

Fearful then of Loingseachan's vengeance, he wandered on, coming at last to the land of the Britons. He held the castle of the king of that land upon his right side and came upon a forest, wherein he heard sounds of lamentation and anguish. Sweeny entered the forest and found there another madman, the Man of the Wood. Each recited the aetiology of his derangment, and the two entered upon a contract of friendship: "Sweeny," said the other, "we have exchanged confidences, now each must be the other's guard; he who attends the crane's call break above the blue and turquoise waters, who hears the lucid cry of cormorants, the clatter of a woodcock's wings, snapping of spent wood, or sees birds' shadows on the roofing boughs, let him give warning; two tree-trunks shall divide us and if either hears any of these things or similar, then let us flee, swiftly."

For a year they were together; then the Man of the Wood had, perforce, to go to where his death awaited him, to be snatched by a gust into a waterfall to drown. He delayed only until Sweeny had told him his own tale just as it is set down hereinafter, then sought out that fatal and elementary conjunction, and the fall included him.

Sweeny went back to Glen Bolcain. There a madwoman pursued him until Sweeny divined her madness and turned, whereupon she fled before him. This he made the subject of his chant, strophe and shrill counterstrophe.

He did not stand. His course brought him back to the home of his old wife Eorann, where again he came to grief; she, seeing his wretchedness, rejected him. On Benn Boirche, a peak among the southern ranges, he found such rest as he could take, victim of storm and graupel, and retold the shifting numbers of his ways.

At firstlight he entered again upon his route; he crossed the green and limpid Shannon, saw the sublime Sliabh Aughty as he made his way to Bile Tiobradain in east Connaught. That night the snow came down, and as it fell it froze, drift upon drift. "Though it be the death of me," said Sweeny, "better to suffer philanthropy than such incessant pain." In this form, a gleam of reason came then to the nearly reclaimed haggard; but it was revealed to Ronan Finn that Sweeny had come to, and would return amongst his people. Adamant through time, the monk renovated his curse: "let him have no relief from your just vengeance, Lord, till death," and the Lord obliged.

At midnight Sweeny halted at the centre of Sliabh Fuaid, and there beheld an apparition. Bloody truncated torsos, their lopped heads leaping beside them, gibbered and brawled on the path, and five of them, heads grizzled and hirsute, lacked torso or trunk between them. He heard their chat:

"He's mad," said the first head.

"A madman of Ulster," said the second.

"Let us hunt him," said the third.

"Long let the hunt be," said the fourth.

"To the sea," said the fifth, and they lifted towards him; headlong he fled.

The call of that hunt was the din and stridulation of stark terror and the hubbub of the chivvying spectres. They butted and plucked at his calves, ankles, shanks, shoulders and nape, clashing with branches, rocks, and each other like a flood unleashed and falling. At last he hid in the high gauze of the clouds, to be sure to be sure that he had lost them; both human heads and those of dog and goat which had been intermingled.

Such was the most strenuous of Sweeny's flights, and for three fortnights after he didn't halt from his career long enough even to drink.

Another of Sweeny's demented journeys took him from Luachair Deaghaidh to where the serene waters of Fiodh Gaibhle doubled its bright blossom. For a year he fed upon the blood-red and the saffron berries of the holly-trees, the dark earth-colours of the acorns, and clear water, then his grief returned upon him and he took up his chant.

He was diverted only briefly then by the cliff of Farannan, but was pleased enough by its ivy and apple-trees, and by the wild deer and the ponderous swine of the valley, and the fat seals snoring on the wrack below, and so he praised it.

Soon he came to where Moling was reading to his students; he lay at the edge of the spring and began to crop the water-cress. The saint greeted him, saying that his arrival was foreknown, as, also, his death in that place. Further, he bound the madman that, however far he might travel by day, each night he would return so that his tale might be set down.

This, for a year, was his routine, and each night he attended vespers with the saint. Moling instructed Muirghil, wife of his swineherd Mongan, to give Sweeny some of each day's milking. It was her habit to thrust her heel into the pat of cowdung nearest her, and fill the depression with new milk; surreptitiously, Sweeny would steal into the vacant yard to lap up the proffered meal.

Muirghil fell out one evening with another woman. Out of sheer spite the other accosted Mongan next day as Muirghil was pouring the milk into the dung and Sweeny watched from the hedge beside. "Coward," she said, "there's a man at your wife in the hedge beyond." The jibe aroused his anger, and he snatched up a spear from the rack and made for the hedge.

Sweeny's flank was towards him as he lay feeding from the dung. The herd lunged, the blade penetrated the rib-cage beside the right nipple and so shattered the spine. Or was it perhaps the tine of a deer's antler which the herd had concealed at Sweeny's trough which did the irreparable harm?

Whichever the case, when the deed was reported to Moling he came with retinue of clerics to the place where Sweeny lay, and there administered all appropriate sacraments.

It was then that the stricken man uttered his final chant as the death-swoon softened him and he could no longer sustain the rigorous discipline of his derangement. He lasted long enough only to be enjambed across the threshold of the church, whereupon death took him. He was interred by Moling with the inevitable rites.

Moling it was who first recorded this tale of Sweeny, and noted his chants, but it is uncertain to how great an extent that saint expressed his reverence for the silent dead by emendation of a strange and confused history, and how far editors and critics have conspired with him, and time, and chance, to make corruption of the word outpace that of the flesh. Perhaps a final turn was added too, to make a palinode. May we, then, conclude just this: that, after all, we have not here those words which Sweeny, between flight and fall, spoke to the Man of the Wood?

I

God has given me life;

without music, without rest,
without woman's company,
loveless
he gave me life,

and so you find me here
living disgraced in Ros Bearaigh;
the life God gave
seems somehow dislocated.

You do not wish to know me.

II

The blackthorn drinks my blood again,
my face bleeds on the sodden wood.

Flood and ebb encompass me;
lunar phases can't affect
the homicidal iron I dread.

Thorns lance my sores. I doze.

III

Is it the cold that wakes me;
can deadly iron draw near through dream?

Here night is palpable. – Listen!
hear the sound of mounted men
thunderous through the echoing wood;
have they my imminent death in mind?

Only the rain throbs on the grass.

IV

My lids still slack,
a year of fearful nights has made them
heavy as lids of gold.

Christ, king of saints, hear me,
this is no fate for a monarch.
What dignity is there in this,
dodging between tree and tree?

My feet are open sores.
Two black suns
burn in my face
and my raw lips pulse
like edges of a wound.

V

This clearing is too open,
without trees;
I am vulnerable here
without spear or shield.

I have no weapons;
I know no women in Glen Bolcain.

Listen to the wind.
No deft fingers jerk the lutestring.

The blackthorn bears new fruit tonight:
an insane king.

His blood becomes its sap,
flowing like water.

VI

I am too weak for wars,
mine is a complete poverty;
snow sits next neighbour to the bone
of pauper and energumen.

There is no further hindrance in the night
which snow-blind eyes anticipate;
ice and wood
have thrown up palisades against me,
blossoms can lacerate the flesh.
Pathways of this dementia
writhe, serpentine, on earth.

My pale paunch juts
from a torn and threadbare vest:
I am Sweeny of Ros Earcain,
call me Sweeny crazed.

The ice-sharp wind lances me through,
the snow has left me red and raw;
upon this gale I drift to death
that dangles from each twisted tree:
fear has enervated me,
left me frenzied in Glen Bolcain.

VII

Madness shrieks beneath my feet
as I search for watercress.

Madness lurks among the reeds
leaping at me when I stoop
about a hill-pool.

Madness has a white and haggard face.

VIII

When the livid sky is swollen with thunder
and the reeds ache beneath the pelting hail;
then you may see the proud, the noble Sweeny
dragging his sodden rags across blue flesh.

IX

In summertime the blue-grey herons stand
rigid above sharp waters.

In wintertime the wolfpacks
thread the snow-glens with their spoor,
and with their moaning they thread the long wind.

I hear their snow-blurred howling
as I cross the iron lakes
and crack the frost from my beard.

X

Frost stands in the air
ice grips the bone;
ice holds half the doubled moon:
snow is coldest
before dawn.

Nothing delays, my love,
decay of crimson cloth.
On bleak plateaux
snow and the wind
undressed me long ago;
cruel sempstress briar
confounds seam and suture,
sews my skin with wood.

Sweeny possessed
is Sweeny dispossessed
of glib and dazzling wife.
Do not, therefore,
distress yourself
who once were
subject of my
sad distraction;
with you, good love,
I harvest tares.

You and the thorn
still mortify
proud flesh.
For a down bed
I am abandoned
and unanswerèd;

the falcon does not brood
upon such mutes.
Chanting, I will stoop and bind
upon a field of air.

Brambles cast
sly nets of wood;
the air is thorned with frost:
before dawn always
wind is sharpest.

XI

You whose thorned orbs fix me
know I am a fallen image;

dulled and scarred since war
is Sweeny, the pre-eminent:

stay house-held and husbanded;
our paths, co-terminal. Woman, I go.

XII

Life is loud in the glen.

Frail stag,
        your cry has halted me;
now I am sick with sudden longing:

odour of herds from pasturelands,
stag bold in crag and sky.

Oak, broad and leafy spire;
good fruit bends the hazel wands.

Gap stopped with dappled boughs,
bright alder boughs;
there are no blood specks on my skin
as I move on.

Blackthorn: barbed wine. And this
above the pool and on the pool, sparse
and sour green,
                cress.

Saxifrage and oyster-grass
are a green path. and see
this ochre, fallen fruit,
this apple-tree.

Mountain blossom. Mountain ash.
My flesh has dropped in a crimson net;
briar, drunk-thorn briar.

Yew is the little churchyard tree,
and where the night of wood congeals
the ensnarled darkness is named 'ivy'.

In hollyboughs I hide from storms,
I hide from the clubbed ash too.

Verge of a dark wood,
vertical chalked motif,
slender, silver, coiling, lovely
birch.

Aspen is swift; its leaves
sing like a distant war;
green blade smashes green blade.
Then, for a time,
                        silence.

In forest glades
my dread:
oakwood pendulous in wind.

XIII

Mountains are rivered slopes,
brown rock and scree;
I would sleep if I were let
in green twilight of Glen Bolcain.

Water; light through green glass,
wind bright as glancing steel,
the ouzel sips the vivid spring,
cress green as the ocean's ice.

Slopes littered with tough ivy,
thin willows blade the mirrored streams,
yews are intense and many there,
birch is the dim glen's lamp.

No act could hold me, Loingseachan;
I would break frosted routes up Boirche.

You were a scabbard of iron words:
father and mother
daughter and son
and brother dead;

supple sweet body,
bright wife
gone to earth.

I am a cave of pain.

XIV

Dense wood is my security,
the ivy has no edge.

Though the lark pursues me,
summed, I take the dove
that crosses, and am no red hawk.
Shadow of the rising woodcock,
blackbird's scream, disturb me.

I stoop to see the little fox
a-worrying of the butchered bones;
he has more shifts to seize me than the wolf.
The guileful fox, the murderous wolf I shun,
scumber and filth befoul them.

Light folds and bends in the chill ice
of pools, and I am cold.
Still, the heron is at sedge,
the badgers squeal in Benna Broc.

Here there are ample stags
to turn much fallow with the share,
but no hand holds
the stag of high Sliabh Eibhlinne,
the stag of sharp Sliabh Fuaid,
the stags of Ealla and of Orrery,
the fierce stag of Loch Lein,
the stag of twin-spurred Baireann;
each stands at rest on salient ground.

Sweeny, I, swift visitant of glens;
rather, call me Man Run Through.

O stag, I could lie down
among your jagged tines
in pointed luxury;
now I await the final point.

See the royal stag go by
dressed in his tattered velvet.

Ronan Finn compelled me here.

XV

My sleep is sad
without feather-bed, numb
from the sharp air
and the grit of the wind-blown snow.

Cold wind with ice,
ghost of an old sun,
shelter of a single tree
on this barren table-land.

Striding through rainstorms,
pacing the mountain deer-paths
and paths through grass
in the orange frost at dawn;
stags are belling
in forest copses,
the paths of the deer are sheer and hard:

I hear the hammer of the distant surf.

O great God above
my weakness is also great
and black are the sorrows of Sweeny
whose scrotum hangs slack.

XVI

Four winds fetch many miles
to meet in me, am as a fifth,
fluent and cold. Boirche
is perilous: so deep
its silent reaches, power
of secret currents threatens me.

I have not yet forgotten
harvest-time in Ulster
around quivering Lough Cuan;

I have lived in Ossory
and within the glades of Meath,
now their springs inhabit me;
in the aftermath of fruit
observe such exaltation:

I sift the debris of the shattered woods.

XVII

I occupy in alien woods
an old retreat;
in my familiar square of trees
shrewd centre of such intimate quincunx am I
whistle of a woken plover
is unsettling plangency.

Secure amid a lasting drift of leaves
I graze on mast and sorrel.
Hazards are these:
shy doves agog in upper branches,
cormorant's disturbance.

Where heron calls cold waters move,
my soft co-occupant of woods.

XVIII

Enmity is sorrow.

Better be stillborn,
better a misbirth, slight sprawling foetus,
than bear enmity.

There is seldom a league of three
but one murmurs;
blackthorn and briar have wounded me
so it is I who murmur.

The crazed woman fears her man;
mine is a curious story,
as the naked man, his feet unshod,
hides from the fearful woman.

When the wild duck and the autumn
move among the glades and lakes,
and the woodlands glow like thickening honey;
then it is good to rest, cradled in the gloom of ivy.

Whosoever bears enmity,
whether man or wife,
whosoever bears enmity,
may he die eternally.

Glen Bolcain has bright waters;
I have heard it loud with birds
and foaming streams
and the lisp of river-surf on reefs.

Holly and the close wands of its hazel
have sheltered me; berries and nuts

acorns and blue velvet sloes,
these have fed me.
Its woods are quick with hounds,
and the stag, at gaze, barks;
all is mirrored in the lucid waters.

I did not hate it.

XIX

My madness finds congruity
on the frozen peak of Boirche;
but what milk or bread sustains
flesh invaded by the snow?

A strait bed sprung with frost
straddles the barren rock,
branches play bone
to wasted limbs.

In a cage of ice
I pace the bars
while frost-buds mimic sweat.

I give fire to the glinting wind.

As the snow succeeds the hail
in autumn I, precipitate,
abandon chasms
of oblique basalt
for zones less igneous,
less cold: replete
anfractuous Glen Bolcain.

Four gaps to the wind
define the glen;
its fertile woods,
its frigid springs
trapped in sheer pits.

Through clear pools gravel spins
in a shifting vortex,

cress and brooklime
dip their leaves
to make a green meniscus.
Beyond, as in, Glen Bolcain
drenched earth tonight is frozen,
but no marauder breaks
the glen's secure horizon.

Bitter leaves
drift among berries there,
garlic and the wild onion
exhale their pungent steam
against the iridescence of the sloes,
and underfoot the path
is frail with acorns.

See, in decaying groves, a king
who stumbles among pawns.

XX

I am miserable
Sweeny,
bone and blood
are dead;
sleepless;
storm-sound
is the only music.

Luachair Deaghaidh
to Fiodh Gaibhle
journeying,
fed on the ivy-crop
and oakmast;
a twelvemonth on this mountain,
aviform,
gorged on the saffron holly-fruit.

Berserk
in Glen Bolcain,
my anguish is
patent,
my strength is worn away tonight,
I have cause for grief.

XXI

Cliff of Farannan,
abode of saints; with many hazel groves
and nuts in cluster; quick icy brooks
that sprinkle down its walls: there are green cords
of ivy, a rich mast of acorns
and the apple-trees,
heavy with good fruit they arc
their boughs.
Many badgers make their setts and the lithe hare
shelters there, the seals gather in
from the open sea.

I am Sweeny,
son of Colman the Just.
I have lain weak
beneath many frostfalls;
Ronan of Druim Gess outraged me.

I shall rest beneath some tree
at that far
waterfall.

XXII

I once thought that the quiet speech
of people held less melody
than the low throating of doves
that flutter above a pool.

I thought the bell
by my elbow not so sweet
as the fluting of the blackbird to the mountain
or the bellow of a hart in the storm.

I thought the voice
of a lovely woman less melodious
than the dawn-cry
of the mountain grouse.

I thought the yowling
of the wolves more beautiful
than the baa and bleat
of a preaching priest.

Though in your chapel you find melody
in the quiet speech of students,
I prefer the awesome chant
of Glen Bolcain's hounds.

Though you relish salted hams
and the fresh meat of ale-houses,
I would rather taste a spray of cress
in some zone exempt from grief.

I am transfixed; the iron
intrudes on shattered bone.

Tell me, God who sanctions all,
why did I survive Magh Rath?

Though each bed I made
without deceit was good
I would rather inhabit familiar stone
above Glen Bolcain's wood.

I give thanks to you, Christ,
for partaking of your body;
in my death I truly repent
all my evil deeds.

Love Songs
from
a
Dead Tongue

•

*Worked from
the Late
Middle-Irish*

for George Hitching

Grief in the king-fort?
With Niall gone, small wonder;
all was fast against affliction,
grievous now.

And will grieve on
abandoned by civility,
though a dynasty outlasted
loneliness from there.

All kings but one
in time relinquish rule.
Who'd want the world?
Grief in the king-fort,
                grief.

Laughter across the way marks out
the marriage-house;
such loud excess
intrudes a desolation here.

Though happily that bride
may get what she contracted for
some are short-changed
as I hereby lay charge.

You, ruler of the lasting world,
I now denounce,
for killing of my kind, my gentle
loving and most innocent king.

As hostage he'd be worth
thoroughbred herds, goldhoards;
who brought him here would learn
my further kindnesses.

Proper to ransom such a man
could to me show him so kind
delivering me from a one-day's raid
some twelve score head of beef.

Delicate linens, ah! you break
my heart, you, where Niall could sleep sound,
and you, white one, little bed,
you miss him too.

How then should I bear myself
happening upon a shirt

when he it dressed
lies dead in Kells?

Travelling westward from Armagh
Niall put me this:
whichever goes in front,
my love, where should we head?

Straight answer, this, my king,
together in the cool clay
of Ailech, let them lay us
in a single grave.

If you, my love, go first,
in front of me into the earth,
I'll take myself no other queen
but long grieving without laughter
                    without laughter.

Kells, occasion for blindness,
since I lay with your king;
Kells, grown disfigured
now Niall is gone.

The first kings I wived,
I augmented their glory,
but Niall was far dearer than both;
Kells, occasion for blindness.

My bright Niall ceased,
my man and my king ceased,
here his broad lands continue;
Kells, occasion for blindness.

Well I remember generous Niall
here on this hill
laughing his wealth away;
Kells, occasion for blindness.

I will walk to the grave of Niall;
there is room where he lies
for me to lie next him;
Kells, occasion for blindness,
                    blindness.

Breaks the heart keening
as the edge keen the king,
keen Niall Blackknee
gracious as great.

[*This is doubtful*]

Ask what breaks my heart:
keening Niall the bright laughing;
till doomsday the heart hurt
atrociously wasting.

First I came into Munster:
high-king's consort queen
to arch-bishop Cormac
the perfectly-bright.

Then next into Leinster
in which rich realm
though some muttered
I did not starve.

[*This transition is difficult*]

. . . came Tara's heir,
that true prince,
successor to arch-kings.

Together we shared
childhood in Tara,
concentric city
of the true promised land.

That destroyer of pastures,
that master of plunder,
that fiercest of men,
deepest red amongst Irish.

The place where he fell
broke my heart
[*this line is lost*]
nor does Donal survive him.

Niall, king, son of kings,
Donal, soft face unfurrowed,
dead detach me from kin,
reduce heart to sheer blood.

I am Gormlaith, the keening:
first husband-king Cormac,
son Donal, fierce Niall,
these three broke my heart.

O King of the stars,
grant mercy to Niall,
O Mary, great queen,
shield this cold keening
               breaks.

Empty, a fort
stands forewarning to others;
such desolation in a palace
just one trick among life's many.

I miss the princes
hospitable and brave
and grieve
through so much emptiness.

Soon the rest
will make joint desolation;
is this not sign enough?
an empty fort;
      empty.

Rag, patched on patch,
why would I blame you?
not one courtly hand
added craft to your stitch.

In Tara once
alongside Niall of Emain,
happily he honoured me:
I drank from his own cup.

In Limerick once
with loving Niall of Ailech,
my clothes spectacular
among the western chieftains.

When his people gathered
to test their foals for speed
I drank as they drank, wine
from fine horn cups.

Seven score women attended us
in these assemblies
as the race was settled
on the green course of my king.

I am a woman of Leinster,
I am a woman of Meath;
ask which land most dear to me:
no zone of those, but my true king's north.

Brambles snare me,
snarl my rags;

thorn no ally,
briar attacks,
      rag.

Mourning Niall I survive;
what pain could exceed this?
surplus such days,
me so disfigured.

Bone-weary tonight, I,
all love-words exhausted;
draped Tara quenched too,
all glamour gone out.

Emain silent and dark
where they played once,
hosts gathered
departed.

Utter silence in Oileach:
no music;
Lough Foyle's speech is hoarse;
disfigured, I die.

To the west to the east
each kingdom enfeebled,
it grieves me
their grief.

Sad this north too
my voice strange to its soldiery;
the south dwindles away,
grief blurs my face.

My king, son of kings,
who gave away gold,

dead, stuns the woods;
grief endures.

King Niall Blackknee, his queen,
master of armies, his consort,
now has gossip for counsel;
do you question my
        mourning?

Ah! grief my own,
Ah! lost my own love,
destroyed in the night
that king's son went down.

Ah! queen's son set below,
Ah! then what future after,
as giving as brave falls
and the field falls waste after?

Ah! true king now dead
that alive was not halt;
this soul fallen in war,
I chant pity and pain
                    Ah!

Here the hound is neglected
till proven,
the unloved
easily slighted.

The crow's black, say I say,
then, white, they say back;
I go wrong, the same say,
whether striding or bowed.

Bleak the hill without trees,
chill the shoulder unfriended,
and empty the weave without issue,
here, don't I know it?

As she finds in love
from one man satisfaction,
no he ever found
but one woman could please.

That king, son of kings, was my pleasure,
most loved and most brave, that most gentle man
stood head against head
with this child of the arch-king.

I a long age since
in this fort of crude strength,
my force fragile, this frail I,
can't abide
       here.

Soft with that foot, Monk,
you stand by a king's side
shovelling covers
on limbs I lay next to.

An age in that dark, Monk,
you've gravelled him down;
an age in his night
he shrinks from the boards.

That son of free giving
earned better than crosses;
sheet him over with stone
but soft with that foot, Monk.

The queen that chants this,
gentle daughter of kings,
craves that stone for her bed-sheet
so soft with that foot, Monk,
                              soft.

Pity the earth constrains you, Niall,
pity us visit your grave!
status and grace stand annulled
now north holds the north's king dead.

A while with the meek,
a while with the mighty;
better than these my while with Niall
who laughed as he drank.

I had banquets with wine,
I had wealth and society;
now Niall walks with saints
what could prevent him Heaven?

Bright but for black knee
Niall had no equal;
such beauty!
the curl, the grey eye.

Now the surge breaks cold,
the wind storms from the west,
generosity sinks to her knees,
the ship shudders.

Fair switches with foul,
harsh wind knows no ceasing,
bud is blasted on branch
just by this death.

Where was joy sits decay;
hard threnody this:

my friend in his blood,
Tara ruined till the world's end,
                    the pity!

Sighing heavy tonight, God!
heaviest yet;
for loss of the son of my own bright Niall
alive I'd walk under the earth.

All friends dwindle and fade
now that Niall is dimmed
the listening ear
hears no laughter.

Note these dead:
father mother and brothers,
and fosterkin, loved and revered,
dead and buried and gone.

Fair one held me high
over vatfulls of gold,
fed me nothing but honey,
count that fair one dead too.

Account also the young
who smiled on my knee
while I gave them a love
as if blood of my blood.

So many have gone
from the yellow-topped earth
yet this grieves me most:
Donal's cheek stroked with clay.

Though weakness and war
hunt the living

this value survives:
the love of the child of your blood.

Sorrow on her
trusts her son
to the care
of the foolish.

Grief on her
sent her son
into chaos
of waters and men.

Donal, son of bright Niall,
and of twelve generations of kings,
those lovers of verse
now past moving.

The child of such ancestry
darkens the sky;
white his hand, white his foot,
my heart heavy
        sighing.

Preach, priest!
with quick benediction
on the great soul
of him, the well-born.

Scholars and clerks
had regard in his reign;
hearsay truly reported
his charity.

Not my boast but Niall's will:
that three hundred horse,
with ten hundred cows
I gave in one day.

Generality dealt with,
his sage sought my gift:
cattle, three hundred head,
cloth, a rich crimson bolt.

I paid off his poets
enough and excess;
may what they then received
serve now his soul.

Sorrow afflict him who sundered us
while yet I lived,
sorrow on him seized my horseman
left me alone.

Sorrow on him struck asunder
my dear friend and myself

would have been in his debt
had he left us as one.

Mark, priest, this my poem,
since a while we are private;
let ear hold what it catch,
then rise, priest, and
                    preach!

Say, three times thirty,
nine times nine, I've loved,
yet if I now loved twenty more
still it wouldn't satisfy.

For Niall I left
all other loves,
desiring his desire;
who might detain me then?

Among assembled warriors
all trophies fell to him;
yet, encountering such straits,
better I'd loved some serf.

Elaborate cloaks, golden rings,
and strings of thoroughbreds;
broad flood run down to drought,
his goods all gone.

Between heaven and earth,
a white dress and a black cloak
now my sole provisioning;
in Kells of the hundred kings, I starve.

North of the church on Sabbath day
instructed by the gentle touch
of the left hand of my king
I, to the abbot's wife, gave goods.

An orb with golden ornament,
fat cows, two score,

a blue Norse hood, a case of horn,
and thirty ounce of gold.

And she, who has them yet,
repaid me them tonight:
two measures of hard oats,
two eggs from her vast clutch.

By him who lit the sun's fire,
if my Niall of the Black Knee lived,
then, you, you minor abbot's twist,
I'd need no eggs from you!

A roan horse,
a cup, and other articles of gold,
I gave her once, and was returned
a cap, a comb, some sundry pretty cloth.

Wretched be the falsely proud,
wretched they who hoard;
before misfortune struck
remember, poets took my gold.

Who would trade horses
for good verse, may God reward;
if I speak well of Niall, think
what could a poet say, for pay!
                          what say?

Wretched to me
my own homeland,
I'd sooner stay in Ulster
conversing with kings.

Through seventeen years
among this aristocracy
they have dealt with me kindly,
rather kinsfolk than strangers.

I and the mountain lark,
of a muchness our nature:
with the wood within reach
she sleeps in the peat-bog.

Getting so much from Niall
what reason to leave him?
that gentle slender-handed man,
unequalled.

[*This development is obscure.*]

. . . .
wretched.

Niall! pray heaven on his soul!
let every priest pray too;
he knew life's worth,
and my heart, lacking him, grows sick.

That wise head the land obeyed
can't cancel now my grief:
such the incalculable loss;
his speech to me was soft.

His speech to me was sweet:
such the incalculable loss;
I have no taste for words
but beating fists unceasingly.

Beating fists unceasingly,
his death my extreme loss;
and though in triumph he went out,
bitter our affliction now.

Bitter our affliction now
the very churches weep for him;
myself can't limit grief
though enemies deride.

Though enemies deride,
though solidarity lend strength,
with Niall laid low
how now live on?

How now live on
lacking passion, joy and song?

Him who withheld no wealth for self
to mourn demeans each woman well.

Niall! pray heaven on his soul!
to survive him is protracted pain,
that stranger to our company
till judgement day:
            Niall!

Lamentation has its season
and right end, even for gentle Niall;
excess has delivered me
to this not life not death.

A time of one and thirty years,
since that king died,
each night I wept him
seven hundred tears.

Last night he, my dead king, came in,
said: put an end to mourning, love,
the Arch-King of the seraphim
grows weary hearing you.

I turned on Niall,
angry as I had never been before,
said: for what cause should that highest King
turn weary from a penitent?

Remember, love, he said,
God set all men in being;
why then would he wish
to overhear them weeping?

Then Niall himself
turned from me, twisting love;
at sight of this I scream aloud,
spring after him.

For some support
I leaned my breast

against a bed-post of smooth yew
which penetrated it, my heart.

Tonight I implore God
grant me surcease in death;
on what road Niall turns
let me turn too.

King husband first
three hundred cows,
two hundred horse
conveyed me.

Then my second husband king,
never to seem outdone
in generosity of soul,
conveyed me double that.

Why should I hide
from my true king, these gifts?
Such gifts, and twice such more,
Niall gave me in one month.
                    Lamentation

**Séan O Duibhir
of
the
Glen**

Through the early sunshine
of this summer morning
hounds raise up their howling
            while the sweet birds sing.
The small beasts and the badger
keep covert with the woodcock,
all lie low from the echo
            and the booming of the guns.
Fox red on rock keeps lookout
on the horsemen's hurly-burly
and the woman by the wayside
            lamenting scattered geese.
But now the woods are levelled
let us leave familiar landmarks
since, Séan, my friend, it's over,
            the game is up and gone.

That's why I sing of sorrow
bone frozen to the marrow
as the north wind comes to winnow
            and death is in the air.
My dog, my dear companion,
is leashed without the freedom
you'd give a child to cheer him
            in the bright noon of the day.
On crags, the royal stag bounding
bears his antlers proudly
and he'll run on through the furzelands
            till the last day of this life;
if I had no more harrassment
from this town's petty gentry
I'd take ship out of Galway
            and leave off these wild ways.

The homesteads of Glen Srutha
lack loft or roof among them,
in Sráid na gCuach a silence
     substitutes for praise;
Harsh weather without shelter
from Cluain to Stuaic na gColm,
the hare beside the headland
     unharried all its days.
What is this human tumult
with so much fell destruction
the sweet thrush and the blackbird
     find no twig for song?
Sure omen of war's onset,
to see priests and people troubled,
driven to harsh havens
     among the upland glens.

My one regret this morning
that I did not die reproachless
that time before the scandal
     caused by my own kind,
when many the long bright evening
saw apples crowd the branches,
when leaves enclosed the oakwood
     and dew was on the grass.
But now I am an outcast,
lonely, far from friendship,
I lodge alone in thickets
     and hollows in the scree;
but unless there's no harrassment
from this town's petty gentry
I'll leave all my possessions
     and so resign my soul.

Two
Anonymous
Love
Songs
from
the
Irish

She is my love
        was most my misery
preferred for wasting me
        to her could cure

She is my fair
        would fast enfeeble me
not whisper for my going oh!
        or mind my grave

She is my dear
        nature's accessory
wouldn't reach a hand to hold my head
        lay me for gold

She is my why
        drops not a hint to me
heeds no true word
        spares no regard

Great is my grief
        too long this lingering
who most suspects me
        is all my love

I will not die for you
O woman like a swan, withdrawn,
You've wrecked your share of fools,
Remember they weren't me.

On what account would you have me wasted?
For the red mouth, is it, or the flowers within?
For the seeming soft, or the swan-like breast?
Tell me, are those to die for?

Those upright breasts, that perfumed skin,
The blushing cheek, the ruffled nape?
Assure yourself I'll never die
For them, God be my help!

Fine your eyebrows, gold your mane,
Safe your secret, slow your speech,
Neat your ankle, smooth your thigh,
But I'm not the fool would die for them.

Sweet your pleasure, your's your choosing,
Slight your palm, like foam your flank,
Blue eye, white throat,
I will not die for you.

O woman like a swan, withdrawn,
I studied with a cunning man.
O slender hand, white throat,
I will not die for you.

I'm not gonna die
little lady
I'm not gonna die
for you
so get used to it

Cos why would I die
if I was gonna die
gimme a good reason
red mouth honey mouth
gimme a break why doncha

Sharp tits sweet skin
don't make the grade
any more little lady
or the blush or the ruff
-led nape no deal

So I'm not gonna sigh
little eyebrow pen
-cilled bottle blonde
for your fashion heel
and your well waxed thigh

Sure you pleasure well
and you know what's what
with your haunch foam
bright and your eye pure
blue but I'm not gonna die

for a milk white throat
or a slender hand—I studied

with a cunning man and I'm not
gonna die for you little lady
no I'm not gonna die today

Cry Help

for Brian Coffey

Cry help? You'll find me fast in my grave first
Who now could come if I did call
since our stronghold our hope our legitimate lord
has himself suffered seizure and failed?

Spun by the rip my mainstay snapped
arse breached with shit bile eats my gut
to see our ground our shelter our wildness our civilized precincts
hocked for a pittance by wasters

Our rivers their frets and divisions stand still
black marshes and palace the Bride and the Boyne
lake sound run red and the ominous seas
since that jack took the tricks from our king

Keen rain
on the road unsettles me
no sound comes near but the roar
of that unstoppable falls

Proud master of salient and hollow of royal demesnes
his stomach is lost with his lands
now the hawk who holds fast those rents and accounts
knows no man as kin

Come down too far from original heights
temporal races fret rockface
where raging headsprings supplement
the river that drops through the settlements

I stop and Death rides up to me
and the dragons are quenched in their courses
and I'm bound to follow my leader down
where His white ledger covers all the deal

A Celticist's Note

The earliest of the Irish-language texts represented here was probably composed in the twelfth century, the latest, in the early eighteenth century. None survives in an original author's hand. Yet the works were transmitted down through the ages in manuscript copies. This scribal tradition did not cease once the Irish poetic tradition began a new life in print. 'Seán Ó Duibhir of the Glen', a song of the seventeenth century, continued to circulate in manuscripts even as text and translation were being published in James Hardiman's *Irish Minstrelsy* of 1831.

The manuscripts witness to a tradition which linked past and present in a unifying whole. One of the surviving copies of the twelfth-century story of Suibne (Sweeny) was made by an eighteenth-century scribe, while in the same century the poet Aodhagán Ó Rathaille, author of the original of 'Cry help', himself transcribed medieval tales. The Gormlaith poems in the present collection were probably composed around the year 1200, but manuscript copies continued to be made even as late as the nineteenth century. Textual evidence suggests that the medieval love-poem 'I shall not die for you' had popular as well as scholarly currency, and both are represented here.

In Irish manuscript culture, scribes not only preserved texts, they also created new redactions. Manuscript collections brought past works into the present, thereby allowing mutual illumination of past and present. A parallel process may be discerned in Trevor Joyce's work. He presents poems which span the Irish poetic tradition from medieval to early modern, and his redactions both represent and re-imagine the Irish originals. New juxtapositions and enlightening associations are created by his work of collection. In the individual poems he is intuitively attuned to the expression of his predecessors, and to the importance of metrical form and of word-play in the Irish compositions. While resounding uniquely, the voices of his poems simultaneously resonate and harmonize with voices in another language and in other times.

Máire Herbert

Author's
Notes

The Poems of Sweeny, Peregrine

In the Irish text 'Buile Suibhne' we may read how Suibhne (Sweeny), while engaged at the Battle of Magh Rath (637 a.d.), fled the fight and became a gealt. A description of this *avis rara* is to be found in the thirteenth-century Norse *Speculum Regale*: 'It happens that when two hosts meet and are arrayed in battle-array, and when the battle-cry is raised loudly on both sides, that cowardly men run wild and lose their wits from the dread and fear which seize them. And then they run into a wood away from other men, and live there like wild beasts . . . then feathers grow on their bodies as on birds. Their swiftness is said to be so great that other men cannot approach them, and greyhounds just as little as men. For these people run along the trees almost as swiftly as monkeys or squirrels.'

The early Irish law tract, the *Book of Aicill*, which may be regarded as a product of the tenth century or earlier, remarks that: 'Suibhne Geilt having become mad is not a reason why the battle [of Magh Rath] is a triumph but it is because of the stories and poems he left after him in Ireland.' It would seem, then, that the tradition of Sweeny's madness and of his poems goes back perhaps to as early as the seventh or eighth century. The text, as it survives, seems somewhat the worse for lacunae and the pious interpolations of monks; the former have at least the virtue of reinforcing the sense of Sweeny's stress and distress. That text has been edited by J.G. O'Keeffe (1913 and 1931) and it is from his labour that this note and the accompanying working have borrowed their small gloss.

The relation in which the 'Poems of Sweeny, Peregrine' stand to the original Irish of 'Buile Suibhne' may perhaps best be described by that phrase which Clarence Mangan used of his own inventive translations: they are 'the antithesis of plagiarism.'

Love Songs from a Dead Tongue

These poems have been worked from Irish originals, some dating back at least to the fifteenth century and perhaps several centuries earlier. They speak in the voice of the famous queen

Gormlaith (d. 948 AD), whose three husbands were all kings, the last being Niall Blackknee who, in 919, died in battle with the Norse. Eleven of the originals are presented with scholarly translation by Osborn Bergin in his *Irish Bardic Poetry* (Dublin: Dublin Institute for Advanced Studies, 1970). An additional six have been drawn from the paper 'Triamhuin Ghormlaithe' by Anne O'Sullivan, published in *Ériu*, vol. XVI (Dublin, 1952).

As far as I am aware this extended sequence of the Gormlaith poems had not previously been published together, either in the original or in translation, prior to my gathering them into this set. I would like to express my thanks to Máire Herbert for her advice and encouragement.

Sean O'Duibhir of the Glen
The Irish text of the seventeenth-century folk-song 'Sean O'Duibhir a' Ghleanna' is available, along with a very free English version by Thomas Furlong, in *Irish Minstrelsy or Bardic Remains of Ireland* by James Hardiman (repr. Shannon: I.U.P., 1971).

Two Anonymous Love Songs from the Irish
Originals of both of these poems are given in *Dánta Grádha: An Anthology of Irish Love Poetry, 1350–1750*, collected and edited by Thomas F. O'Rahilly (repr. Cork: Cork UP., 1976). The second also occurs, with translation, in *Love Songs of Connacht* by Douglas Hyde (repr. Shannon: I.U.P., 1968).

'Cry Help' was worked from the Irish of Aogán O'Rathaille (c. 1675–1729).